The Space Between

Poems by
ANNA ELKINS

© 2013 Anna Elkins

w o r d b o d y
PO Box 509
Jacksonville, OR 97530

All rights reserved. No part of this book may be reproduced in any form or by any means without permission in writing from the author except in the case of brief quotations embodied in articles or reviews.

Cover image: "What is the Space Between Two People?" by Anna Elkins

Cover design by Anna Elkins

ISBN-13: 978-0615891415
ISBN-10: 0615891411

Harbor hopes as big as ships equipped to cross worlds.

CONTENTS

Part I: What Is 7
    Meanwhile 8
    Invitation 9
    C.V. 10
    Shore Hymn, Sotto Voce 11
    The Shape of Taste 12
    Crossings 14
    Now 15
    Yields 17
    The Fig of It 18

Part II: What Is Dreamed 19
    Down to Sleep 20
    The Usual 21
    The While of Thaw 22
    In which a Ship's Figurehead Turns Outside-in 23
    If Sky Is Skin, then What Is Wind? 24
    To Readers of Ecclesiastes 25
    Terrarium Dweller 26
    The Birth of History 27
    Found 28

Part III: What Is Dreamed of in Day 29
    This Side of Night 30
    The Princess and the P(atience) 31
    The Who of Day 33
    In the Tradition of Mystics I 34
    In the Tradition of Mystics II 35
    Fathoming 36
    The Long Sleeve of God 38
    To What Comes 40
    For Those Who Walk Between 41

Acknowledgements *42*

PART I:
WHAT IS

Meanwhile

The space between fingers speaks
to the space between lips
between letters
between worlds.

There is nothing sweeter than this distance.

Meanwhile, be a rose of closeness.
I am the shape of waiting.
Trace the contour of my heart—
it curves and ducks and swerves.

Be the heart-shaped roads I run
to keep strong
to find a way closer to you.

In between
I wait
all the mean while.

Invitation

Fog rests in the forest, hiding
a world between grass and branches—
a world so soft and molecular
that breath would end it.

Once, I was invited to a back room.
A man opened a drawer, then a box,
then a folio with a spine thick as my fist.
He turned to a page bold in gold leaf.
I could see my face in the burnished
brightness. I leaned over, breathed *Oh* . . .
The man shook his head. I might
dull that brilliance with a breath.

Oh, fragility kept pressed
behind pages, boards, box, drawer—
robbed of light. How can the story
shine if not exposed to the elements
that could destroy it?

Walk in this winter.
Wave your arms and holler
until you see your own breath.

C.V.

Karlsruhe, Germany

I am the door and the ear against it.

I am the pin and the skin it nicks.

I am the towel and the seconds before it's dry.

I am the dredges and the bottom of the cup they settle in.

I am Saturday kissing Sunday.

I am the postcard and the day it isn't sent.

I am the edge and the belly.

I am the clasp and the day it breaks.

Shore Hymn, Sotto Voce

All stones are broken stones — James Richardson

To know ourselves like stones, sure
of every curve & gravell'd belly.

To wear prayer crossing
our bodies in arms of agate.

To take pain for the shaping
& sanding away of faults & pits.

To become palmable softness, smooth
weight warming in the grace of a hand.

The Shape of Taste

These almonds have come to me
from a country I'll visit soon.
Perhaps I'll pass by the tree
whose fruit I'm tasting—
salty and blanched and traveled.
Did the roots begin
their soily descent when
Santiago made his famous way,
sea-shelled, across the Pyrenees?
Did centuries of branches rise toward skies
until they burst into blossomed song?
Did leaves praise the same source
the pilgrims wandered for?

Those sandaled *peregrinos*
live on in frescos. I met one once.
He walked, locked in paint,
toward a cloistered door—
caught wanting always to leave.
Above him, a Madonna and child
ascended to a brickless heaven,
drawn in a mandorla—
the almond crossection
of two, overlapping circles.
Two, overlapping worlds.

Heaven tastes earth,
earth bites back.

I finish my almonds, eating
each tree
each entry to eternity
each man and woman who sought
beyond their walls.

I am full.
I have consumed the seeking world.

Crossings

Germany, 2001

My train slows through a weedy crossing
where children wait, holding their bikes
at angles under their short bodies, twisting
the handles right and left. I catch the eyes
of a small boy with white tires. Before he blinks,
I've imagined his house up the road and me in it:
frying pan still warm from the breakfast eggs
I just cooked. His bin of building blocks empty,
yesterday's castle still commanding the middle
of the living room. I will leave it for him to come
home to. He can still feel the washcloth I used
to rub his fingers clean of honey and mud. But just
as he blinks, I look away, and we both know I am nothing
near mother and am not regretting it. These eyes
don't soften and ask *Did you sleep good, baby?*
Where's that dirty shirt from yesterday? Too many
miles between his pedal-itching feet and me
in this graffiti'd, backward-facing seat, watching
the curved body of my train pass an anonymous
knot of children, car after car after car.

Now

California, 2011

I once wrote about a boy on a bike
glimpsed through a train window,
how he looked at me like a son to a mother,
how I stared, distant, back.
That poem acts as prophetic cement
I wish to crack
not with hammer but with a tree of life
grown slowly beneath, its roots now thick
enough to break what I have poured.

Now, the train is moving backward.
I look through time and graffiti'd window.
I wave to the boy. He lifts his hand
from handlebars and waves back,
turning into a man old enough
to be a father
to see me not as mother
but as the last brink of girl before
irrevocably woman.

Here I am
hands to abdomen
as my cycle sheds another life
I came into this world with.
To you who may remain:

Call your father to me

Call from where you wait to try this earth
Call him to me

I want to carry you into this crazy place
of wheels and why's.
Cry out with me, loud enough
for your somewhere-father to hear.
Seat him beside me on this train.
I'll take over from there,
I promise.
You live behind our kiss.
Help me make this word-reversal true:
now life has *won*.

Yields

We learn what 1 x 1 2 x 1 3 x 1 equal.
We learn that any 'o' after that 'x' means
nothing.

I ask of math: set an equal sign after all
the letters and numbers
I've stacked a life with.
Set that sideways pair of lines right here,
after the scramble of my parentheticals
and square roots.
Double-lined sign, sweet equalizer,
symbol of two sides congruent —
link me with one whose own math
equals my yield.

O for the answered equation.
O for the mathematician to solve it across
the broad whiteboard of daytime sky.
O for us to see our lives united —
clouds moving the unproven,
rain washing away the un-functions,
and sun burning through the zeros
until all it shines on is an equal sign.

Look, the sign is turning.
Look, it's standing right-side-up.
Look, it's the two of us speaking
the universal language of the heart.

The Fig of It

I find a fig tree circled
by its own fallen fruit.
The carpet of rot permits me
to pull a soft, ripe drop
of sweetness and eat.

O, audible flavor!
The fig's each seed
tells the mouth a story
of what may grow
with right soil, light, and rain.

Each seed of my life
asks to grow, tended, into
a useful, beautiful yield.
Each seed blooms toward fruit
with every hope of sharing
its own reward.

I mourn small losses:
figs that missed
a table of friends & cheese,
figs that won't know
the steep of time, jarred
'til winter hunger wakes them.

Make my life this:
a ready harvest
given, taken, tasted.

PART II:
WHAT IS DREAMED

Down to Sleep

On the brink of sleep,
prayers dissolve like salt
in water. Each shape
of blessing, praise, favor
is lost, but every flavor
comes to the tongue,
turns into savor of night—
sour and faithful
to return the next morning.
The soul to keep.

The Usual

Today, like any other day, I fell
from heaven, drank a river,
and swallowed a world
(it tasted like beets & sweet tea).

Today, like any other day,
the roads lifted off the earth
and danced in cement-y ribbons,
asking me to fly.

Today, like any other day, I held
the sky to my heart
and felt the heavens breathe
(it sounded like stars singing).

The While of Thaw

By morning, winter night has turned
into a bird — its plumage spread wide
in ice across the windshield.

I climb inside the car and sit,
looking through a crystal matrix
that repatterns sky and trees.

I wait with this feathered bird of freeze
for the sun to melt us into motion,
that we might see where we're heading.

In which a Ship's Figurehead Turns Outside-in

My ship points inward
like a sleeve stuck
inside a shirt. Any
limb will reach core.

My cargo is heart,
heaven. The weight
so light, it almost
flies, this vessel.

Yes. See beneath me?
Stars. Here I plot
course, planetless.
Orbit with me. Hold

the north-pointing compass.
Tell me when it'll be
too bright to read,
then kiss me with sleep.

I wake, seams back
inside, sleeves filled
with reasonable arms
holding reasonable things:

a bowl of stars
as souvenirs.

If Sky Is Skin, then What Is Wind?

Bruising, the heavens. Filling
with blood-sun, darking to stars.

Sky. Largest organ of earth, of flesh.
Our bodies ripen and line beneath it.

What if we ran around skinless,
bearing our innards like gifts?
All hearts the same, thumping color.

If we claimed the clouds cause us,
every gasping dragon in them?

Seasons slough above
while what covers our bodies—

scarable, elastic case
for knuckles and blood—shifts too.
Our sky it is, in slim disguise.

To Readers of Ecclesiastes

L'Abri: Huémoz, Switzerland

there is sky in us
    whether or not
    we wear wings

we are born to fly
    no strangers
    to flight
    or desire

it is easy to mistake the pull
    and beat of wing
as meaningless

    perhaps we misread
    perhaps
it is only meaning less
    than the words we cannot taste
    with the flavors of this world

Terrarium Dweller

A glass castle sits in my windowsill
with a young vine inside.
The sun, hot outdoors, pours in.
The plant starts to sweat.
What does the small, green life
think of me that I don't water her
but let the sun begin its work?
She begins to drip,
and just as she thinks the heat's
impossible, her wilting leaves see a leg
of condensation run down a wall, then
another another another
until the whole, clear cage is raining,
and the shoots drink, the roots drink,
even the viney heart & mind drink,
and the plant can't remember ever
being undrenched, and the sun
becomes a distant friend
blurred to brightness, refracted
through every pendant drop
of an inexplicable quenching.

The Birth of History

What if our world has kept
to one side of the sun
has been turning so slowly
that its farthest continents
have only known the night?

Look, this rusty axis
starts a visible spinning.
Entire kingdoms open
their eyes and blink
at their first mornings.
All the people within them
lift from amber'd sleep.

They wake with stories
told from dreamscapes.
The gravity of narrative
pulls them together.
Shared myths turn history,
and soon, there was always
light, there was always day—
we just had not opened
our eyes to see it.

Found

Saipan, Northern Mariana Islands

Find us, night,
on the edge of the world,
watching
waves beg for day.

We raise our voices
to be heard above the sea
to be heard at all.

Listen, something's singing
Listen, someone's said
that morning's only coming
if we give up night instead

Find us, day,
holding hands
wide open
to the sky

waiting
wading
in the dark.

PART III:
WHAT IS DREAMED OF IN DAY

This Side of Night

What if love
snuck up on you
like your shadow
like your age
like your own voice
waking you in the night
from a dream
so deep
you couldn't breathe
without bringing
it into day?

The Princess and the P(atience)

You, beneath the stack
of mattresses of my life,
I feel your persistence
at every restless angle I lay.

Enough.

* * *

It took a while, hefting
each weighty haste away.
But there you were.

And out the door
I threw you, out
into the wide world
where earth, waiting,
took you in,
covered you up.

I didn't know
you'd take root
right outside my house.

* * *

Now I practice you,
in your again invisible
presence. Now I feel you,
not with body

but with spirit.

This time, I will not
wake to you — a vague
discomfort — below me.
This time, you will wake me
some morning, your
heaven-drenched
branches grown through
my window, your blossoms
on my cheek,
and I will rise — kissed
by the beauty
you have become.

The Who of Day

Each night I pull the large,
square cushions from the head of my bed.
Beneath them hides
the small pillow I sleep on.

Each morning, after distant dreams,
I return to my body and bed.
I return those big cushions
and lean against them
with my morning coffee.

The little pillow hides all day.
It is the owl of my bedding,
sleeping while sun fills my room,
emerging when it's time for night.
When I rest my neck into its softness,
I can see what it dreamed the day long —

The physics of rivers
The flight of fancies

I'm tickled by its feathers of memory.

When the owl asks his ritual *who?*
I answer *I*.
Do I mean the *I* of day?
Do I mean the *I* of night?

In the Tradition of Mystics I

You are the gold I try to shape
into a brick to stack,
but you keep melting.
I can't keep you in a shape to store.
You run over me like honey,
and I am transformed.
Everything I touch turns to you.

In the Tradition of Mystics II

I wake with songs in my soul,
in my body. I redefine organ music:
my lungs, my liver, my heart—
each bit of blood and water is a note
I hold for you.
I call my body
to perpetual song.

Fathoming

The surf rolls in — salty carpet
reaching from land to sea,
from shallow to deep.

The surface — lush —
is a tidal invitation to a place
free of gravity and balance —
a place sourced so far down
no color is visible there.
Or else, so far down
I'd hear a new world
where color is sung
from an audible stage.

Roll in, white carpet, roll out.

I step into it.
Night happens.
The cameras called stars
begin to flash
onto darking waters
I wade — wilder — in, on.

I want not to sink.
I want to walk
in a suspending trust.

I, hovercraft of self,
cross the top of this sea,

unsinkable, unthinkable
that doubt could ever
creep between my toes.

And if it did,
and when it does,
those promised depths await,
sounding blue
in the singing theater
at the heart of the world.

The Long Sleeve of God

For Ishi & Nicci via Lois & Geri

I can only do this
in a poem—take the invisible,
wrap it thick with words,
and see the shape it takes.

It turns into a sleeve
up which history reaches—
wrist to pit.
Whether or not God

wears sleeves,
He's got tricks up there.
I get to believe
they are good ones.

I do.
I've seen Him pull friends
and destinies from that
fabric of heaven.

I've seen Him pull out
everything
from cups of coffee
to continents.

Now I trust for the tricks
I don't even know

to wait for.
I do know to wait.

Up His long sleeve,
all the promises are *yes*.

To What Comes

Applegate Valley, Oregon

I love you as if
you were the yellow rose
growing beside
the guesthouse door
I do not have.

You are the imagined
scents of late summer—
edge of pond,
squash blossom,
madrone bark, peeling back.

You are the love
I wait to wake to
from a deep
and forgotten dream.

You are the dance
I have yet to accept
in a fairytale waiting
to be told.

You are the ring of wine
resting at the heart
where glass meets stem—
everything else
already consumed.

For Those Who Walk Between

Love, sweet alias for the world
we wish to see, come rest
on our heads, close as hair.
Be the reason for the scalp's
work — to grow strands that lift
with the physics of angels.

Love, guide the white.
Give us the wisdom
we cannot reach
but which reaches us —
like a mother bending down
to lift up her child.
Her touch is tonsure —
marks us as those
who walk between.

ACKNOWLEDGMENTS

I thank the editors of the following publications, where some of these poems previously appeared:

The Furnace Review
The Greensboro Review
Grey Sparrow Press
Munitionsfabrik
North Carolina Literary Review
Verdad

Thanks also to:

The Center for Art and Media Technology in Karlsruhe, Germany, for using the poem "C.V." in a sound installation

Composer Cole Bratcher for setting to music the poem "In which a Ship's Figurehead Turns Outside-in" (performed for the Seattle Composers Salon)

And the readers of this manuscript in its various stages: the inimitable Pam Spinosi, the dexterous Joella Skilleter, and the gifted poet-editor, Amy Calkins

To see the art, writings, and et ceteras
of Anna Elkins, visit:
annaelkins.com

www.ingramcontent.com/pod-product-compliance
Lightning Source LLC
Chambersburg PA
CBHW031507040426
42444CB00007B/1236